NEW LOOK

Beginnings and Endings

Henry Pluckrose

Photography by Steve Shott

Watts Books

London • New York • Sydney

Let's begin with a thought.
Most things have a beginning.
Each day begins with a sunrise ...

and ends with a sunset,
the beginning of the night.

Spring is the season at the beginning of the year.

Winter is the season
at the year's end.

‘Start’ means the same as ‘begin’.
We do not start school
when we are grown up …

or go to work
when we are
very young.

Beginnings are
important.
You do not
begin to dress
by putting on
your shoes –
and then
your
socks.

If you did
you might end up
looking like this!

Let's have another thought.
Many things have ends.
Your hair …

coils of rope . . .

and even balls of wool.

Sometimes an end has a particular use. Why do we only sharpen one end of a pencil?

Which end of the
spoon do you
use to eat
your food?

Some things have ends
which look the same ...

even though they
may face in
different directions.

Sometimes an end is a beginning.
This train ends its journey at the station.

When it starts again it is beginning a new journey.

This is the end of the road.
Could it also be the beginning?

This is the end of the land.
It is also the beginning of the sea.

Some things have
no beginning
and no end –
like this bicycle
chain ...

and this
necklace.

Another thought.
We have reached the end of the book!

About this book

This book has been prepared for use in the home, playgroup, nursery and infant school.

The world in which young children grow and develop is a fascinating place. New experiences – things tasted, touched, heard, smelt and seen – crowd one upon another. Such experiences are the key to understanding, for their very richness and diversity fosters curiosity and encourages questioning.

We express our discoveries, our ideas and our thoughts through words. Without language, thoughts could not be shared nor ideas deepened and clarified. This marriage of words with first-hand experience is one of the keys to intellectual development.

Children view the world from a different eye level to adults yet spend their formative years in an environment specifically created for adults. This book, along with its companions in the series, is a visual exploration of everyday life from the child's viewpoint. The photographs and the text encourage talk and personal discovery – both vital elements in the learning process.

Henry Pluckrose

About the author

Henry Pluckrose is a very well known educationalist and respected author of many information books for young people. He is a former primary school headmaster who is now an educational consultant for different organisations at home and abroad.

Watts Books
96 Leonard Street
London EC2A 4RH

Franklin Watts Australia
14 Mars Road
Lane Cove
NSW 2066

UK ISBN: 0 7496 1892 2

10 9 8 7 6 5 4 3 2 1

Editor: Annabel Martin
Design: Mike Davis

A CIP catalogue record for this book is available from the British Library

Dewey Decimal Classification: 600

Printed in Malaysia